Y0-BQS-911

This book is dedicated to my wonderful husband,
Ryan, with love and gratitude.
You are my sunshine, my rainbow leaves,
my candy-colored lights, and my buttercups!

The Little Gnome arrived in
an enchanting Victorian garden
on a warm and beautiful day. The sun
was shining, the flowers were blooming,
and the Little Gnome was smiling.

Happy as could be, the Little Gnome loved
listening to the sweet sounds of the birds singing
and the wind whispering. He felt he must live
in the most perfect garden in the world!

The Little Gnome often awoke early in the morning. He would bask in the warm sunbeams at dawn and rest in the cool shade of the neighboring maple tree in the afternoon.

At night he would watch the big white moon glowing
and gaze happily at the stars.

Woodland friends visited the Little Gnome in the charming garden each day. Playful squirrels searched for berries, hard-working bees collected pollen from the flowers, and boisterous geese splashed in the garden pond. In the air, beautiful butterflies floated on the wind, and bluebirds took their babies for flying lessons.

The Little Gnome absolutely adored his delightful garden friends. He drank in the delicious warm weather and sunny skies. He even enjoyed the cool rainfall on hot afternoons.

After many weeks, he began
experiencing things that he'd never
seen or felt before. It started getting cooler.
He noticed that the sun woke up later and
went to bed earlier. The leaves on the maple tree
began changing from forest green to golden
yellow, mulberry purple, crimson red, and pumpkin orange.

The colorful leaves on the tree soon turned brown
and fell to the ground all around the Little Gnome.

He looked at the crunchy leaves and wondered
if the tree was ill. It was cold now and his
friends didn't visit as often.

All the flowers were gone, too.

The Little Gnome awoke with a shiver one extra-cold morning and was surprised when the sky started sprinkling icy white powder. The mysterious white stuff was quickly covering the ground around the Little Gnome's frozen feet. He was sad to be alone with the frosty white blanket up to his waist.

Shivering in the snow, the Little Gnome was grumpy. He longed for the days when he enjoyed the company of his animal friends in the warmth of the sun. He didn't like these changes and he wished they would go away.

One cold, blustery night in the garden, the Little Gnome heard laughter. He excitedly looked around to determine where the giggles were coming from, but didn't see anyone. Just that moment, the bushes and trees illuminated with thousands of candy-colored lights!

The Little Gnome had never experienced anything like this before. The lights were so wonderful and beautiful that he forgot about the cold.

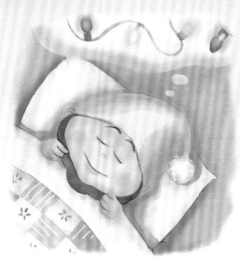

He went to sleep with a joyful smile on his face and in his heart. Each night the spectacular lights reappeared and the Little Gnome delighted in them. He looked forward to it every day and marveled at their beauty until he fell asleep at night.

Then one evening, the beautiful lights mysteriously disappeared. The Little Gnome was sad and grumpy again and wondered why they went away. Every night he waited with anticipation, but they were gone.

After many snowy nights and frigid days, the sun began to get up earlier and stay up later. Slowly the blanket of snow melted and the green grass returned. The Little Gnome was happy to see vibrant yellow buttercups peeking up through the lawn.

Gradually the days grew warmer. The Little Gnome was
overjoyed when his friend Goose splashed down in the
pond nearby. The Little Gnome was excited to have
a friend in the garden again. He described to Goose
all the puzzling changes that had been happening.

Goose giggled and explained the four seasons to the Little Gnome. He told him that the one with the leaves is

 Fall.

The Little Gnome was especially curious about the magical lights he had seen. Goose told him they were the bright lights of the holiday season, part of

Winter.

His friend assured him that Spring flowers would always come back after Winter

 and that hot, sunny Summer days would always return after Spring.

The Little Gnome felt warm and tingly inside as he understood and appreciated the seasons for the first time. He was very excited that the fragrant flowers and all of his fun-loving friends would soon return.

As Spring bloomed around the garden, the Little Gnome was delighted to be reunited with his friends. He relaxed in the cool shade of the maple tree's fresh new leaves dancing in the gentle breeze.

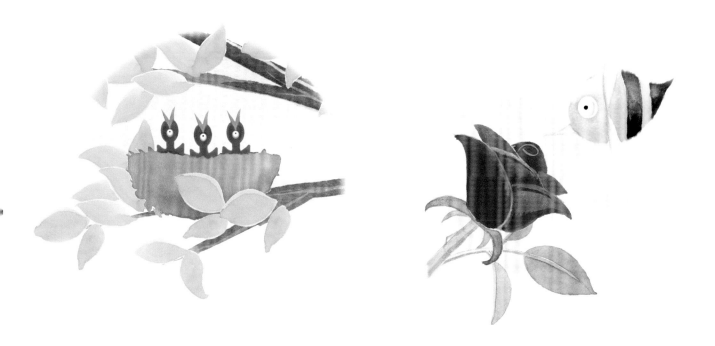

The Little Gnome thought about each of the seasons and how he didn't like the changes at first. He smiled while remembering the rainbow leaves and the colorful lights. He looked forward to enjoying them when the days grew short again.

The Little Gnome now understood that there's something to look forward to and celebrate in every season. From that day forward, he was happy to be a part of them all and lived happily ever after!

Just like the Little Gnome, you can choose to look for the good in every season and situation. When you look for the positive in every change, you will always find something to appreciate and enjoy.